COMPLETE GUIDE TO SNAIL FARMING

Expert Tips, Profitable Techniques, And Sustainable Practices For Successful Heliculture

GIOVANNI MALAKAI

© [2024] [Giovanni Malakai]. All rights reserved.

Except for brief quotations included in critical reviews and certain other noncommercial uses allowed by copyright law, no part of this publication may be reproduced, distributed, or transmitted in any form or by any means, including photocopying, recording, or other electronic or mechanical methods, without the publisher's prior written permission. Write to the publisher at the address below, addressing your letter to the "Attention: Permissions Coordinator," requesting permission.

DISCLAIMER

This book's content is solely intended for informational and educational purposes. The author and publisher of this book make no express or implied representations or warranties of any kind regarding the completeness, accuracy, reliability, suitability, or availability of the information, products, services, or related graphics contained in it, even though every effort has been made to ensure their accuracy and dependability. You consequently absolutely assume all risk associated with any reliance you may have on such material.

The author's own experiences and studies serve as the foundation for the techniques and procedures covered in this book. They might not be appropriate for every circumstance or person. Before putting any advice or recommendations from this book into practice, readers should use their own discretion and take into account their unique situation. Consulting with qualified professionals who specialize in veterinary care and animal management is always a good idea. Any direct, indirect, incidental or consequential damages resulting from using or relying on the material in this book are disclaimed by the author and publisher. Any decisions made by the reader based on the information presented herein are at their own risk.

TABLE OF CONTENTS

CHAPTER ONE 13
  INTRODUCTION TO SNAIL FARMING 13
    KNOWING THE FUNDAMENTALS OF SNAIL FARMING 13
    THE REASONS SNAIL FARMING IS A SUCCESSFUL BUSINESS 14
    ESSENTIAL EQUIPMENT AND TOOLS REQUIRED 15
    MAIN ADVANTAGES OF RAISING SNAILS 16
    TYPICAL MYTHS AND FALSE BELIEFS REGARDING SNAIL 17

CHAPTER TWO 19
  BEGINNING THE SNAIL FARMING PROCESS 19
    SELECTING APPROPRIATE SNAIL SPECIES 19
    RECOGNIZING THE ENVIRONMENT AND SNAIL HABITATS 20
    FUNDAMENTAL SNAIL ANATOMY AND PHYSIOLOGY 22
    ORGANIZING YOUR AREA FOR SNAIL FARMING 23
    SAFEGUARDS AND SANITATION PROCEDURES FOR SNAIL 24

CHAPTER THREE 27
  SETTING UP YOUR FARM FOR SNAILS 27
    HOW TO PREPARE AND CHOOSE SOIL 27
    BUILDING SNAIL HIDES AND PENS 28
    SELECTING MEAL PLANS AND FEEDING TECHNIQUES 30
    WATERING SNAIL SYSTEMS 31
    CONTROL TECHNIQUES FOR PREDATORS AND PESTS 33

CHAPTER FOUR 35
  CONTROLLING SNAIL PROCREATION 35
    COMPREHENDING THE MATING BEHAVIOR OF SNAILS 35

    PROCEDURES FOR LAYING AND INCUBATING EGGS 36

    TAKING CARE OF YOUNG SNAILS AND HATCHLINGS 37

    PHASES OF GROWTH AND DEVELOPMENT 39

    BREEDING STRATEGIES TO BOOST YIELD 40

CHAPTER FIVE 43

  MANAGEMENT OF HEALTH AND DISEASE 43

    COMMON SNAIL ILLNESSES AND PARASITES 43

    SIGNS AND PROMPT METHODS OF IDENTIFICATION 44

    EFFECTIVE PREVENTION AND TREATMENT TECHNIQUES 46

    PROCEDURES FOR SICK SNAILS IN QUARANTINE 47

    VETERINARY ADVICE AND TREATMENT 49

CHAPTER SIX 51

  GATHERING AND HANDLING SNAILS 51

    ASSESSING THE MATURITY OF SNAILS FOR HARVESTING 51

    HUMANE AND ETHICAL HARVESTING METHODS 52

    SNAILS BEING CLEANED AND READY FOR THE MARKET 53

    METHODS OF PROCESSING FOR VARIOUS PRODUCTS 55

    GUIDELINES FOR PACKAGING AND STORING 56

CHAPTER SEVEN 59

  HOW TO PROMOTE AND SELL YOUR SNAILS 59

    CHOOSING THE MARKET YOU WANT TO ENTER 59

    BUILDING A NAME FOR YOUR PRODUCTS MADE FROM SNAILS 60

    PROFITABILITY-DRIVEN PRICING STRATEGIES 61

    NETWORKS OF DISTRIBUTION AND SALES CHANNELS 63

    RELATIONSHIP MANAGEMENT WITH CUSTOMERS 64

- CHAPTER EIGHT 67
  - REGULATORY AND LEGAL ASPECTS 67
    - LICENSES & PERMITS FOR SNAIL FARMING 67
    - OBSERVANCE OF SAFETY AND HEALTH REGULATIONS 68
    - IMPACT ASSESSMENTS AND ENVIRONMENTAL REGULATIONS 70
    - PROTECTION OF INTELLECTUAL PROPERTY FOR INNOVATIONS 71
    - REQUIREMENTS FOR BUSINESS REGISTRATION AND TAXATION 73
- CHAPTER NINE 75
  - GROWING YOUR SNAIL FARMING ENTERPRISE 75
    - BOOSTING THE CAPACITY OF PRODUCTION 75
    - RECRUITING AND OUTSOURCING SUPPORT 77
    - SYSTEMS FOR MANAGING INVENTORY EFFECTIVELY 78
    - BUDGETING AND FINANCIAL PLANNING 80
    - STRATEGIES FOR EXPANSION AND UPCOMING GROWTH 82
- CHAPTER TEN 85
  - FAQS & TROUBLESHOOTING 85
    - TYPICAL OBSTACLES SNAIL FARMERS FACE 85
    - SOLVING ISSUES WITH SNAIL FARMING 86
    - FAQS REGARDING METHODS OF SNAIL FARMING 88
    - PROFESSIONAL SUCCESS SUGGESTIONS AND GUIDANCE 89
    - COMMUNITY RESOURCES AND ASSISTANCE 91
- CHAPTER ELEVEN 93
  - UPCOMING DEVELOPMENTS AND TRENDS 93
    - NEW TECHNOLOGY FOR SNAIL AGRICULTURE 93
    - ECO-FRIENDLY METHODS FOR SNAIL AGRICULTURE 94

CONSUMER PREFERENCES AND MARKET TRENDS 96
RESEARCH OPPORTUNITIES AND EDUCATIONAL INITIATIVES 98
WORLDWIDE PROSPECTS FOR SNAIL PRODUCERS 99

ABOUT THE BOOK

For those who are new to or experienced in snail farming, the "Complete Guide to Snail Farming" is an invaluable resource that provides in-depth knowledge of every aspect of this growingly lucrative industry. The book starts by going over the basics and then highlights how profitable snail farming can be, as well as how it can be a sustainable and fulfilling endeavor.

Giving farmers a thorough rundown of all the tools and equipment they need, gives them the knowledge they need to run their businesses effectively right away.

The main goal of the article is to debunk common myths and misconceptions regarding snail farming so that readers can approach the project with confidence and clarity. The book then dives into useful guidance on choosing the best kinds of snails, comprehending their ecosystems, and setting up ideal farming conditions. Comprehensive talks about the anatomy of snails, how to prepare the soil, and how to build appropriate pens highlight how careful planning is necessary for snail farming to be successful.

In addition, the guide covers important topics like feeding plans, ways to manage pests, and efficient reproduction. Through proactive disease control and veterinary care, it provides farmers with strategies for raising healthy snails through several growth phases and reducing frequent health risks. By placing a strong emphasis on humane harvesting and processing methods, the book helps farmers prepare snails for the market while adhering to ethical norms, which improves the quality of the final product and builds consumer confidence.

Farmers may effectively identify target consumers, build strong brands, and negotiate legal and regulatory frameworks by placing a significant emphasis on marketing and sales tactics. Comprehensive segments on optimizing operations, devising a financial strategy, and resolving typical obstacles enable farmers to grow their enterprises sustainably and take advantage of new market trends and technological advancements in snail farming.

"Complete Guide to Snail Farming" is a vital resource for anybody hoping to succeed in this exciting and dynamic field because it offers thorough advice on everything from initial setup to long-term growth methods.

CHAPTER ONE

INTRODUCTION TO SNAIL FARMING

KNOWING THE FUNDAMENTALS OF SNAIL FARMING

The practice of rearing land snails especially for human consumption or economic gain is called "snail farming," or "heliciculture." It entails building an appropriate habitat—usually with proper humidity and temperature control—that emulates the natural habitat of snails. It's important to understand the snail life cycle since, from egg hatching to adulthood; each stage needs a different set of environment and care to promote healthy growth and reproduction. Beginners should concentrate on choosing the appropriate species for farming, such as the well-known Achatina species, which are noted for their quick development and high rate of reproduction.

Appropriate housing is the first step toward successful snail farming. Conditions with adequate ventilation, a reasonable humidity level, and safety from predators are ideal for the growth of snails.

Simple wooden boxes or plastic containers filled with dirt can serve as housing, or more complex arrangements such as pens with mesh sides to keep off intruders can be used. Providing well-balanced food is crucial. Being herbivores, snails consume a wide range of fresh, green plants, including fruits, lettuce, and cabbage.

THE REASONS SNAIL FARMING IS A SUCCESSFUL BUSINESS

Snail farming is a viable prospect for both personal use and business because of its low initial expenses and strong demand. Snails are becoming more and more popular around the world due to their growing nutritional value and culinary appeal.

Both novice and seasoned farmers can engage in snail farming because of its low space needs and adaptability to a variety of climates. Furthermore, snails can generate several harvests in a year due to their rapid reproduction and short gestation period.

From an economic standpoint, snail farming can provide a consistent flow of revenue by selling directly to customers, restaurants, or wholesale marketplaces. Snails are regarded as a delicacy in some areas and fetch high prices, creating a profitable niche business. Furthermore, because of its moisturizing and anti-aging qualities, snail slime is highly prized in cosmetics, giving farmers who can prepare and market it an extra source of income.

ESSENTIAL EQUIPMENT AND TOOLS REQUIRED

Basic tools and equipment are needed to start a snail farm to protect the health and well-being of the snails. Gardening tools like trowels, rakes, and watering cans are necessary for growing and gathering snail food. For housing snails, farmers also want sturdy, hygienic containers or pens with sufficient ventilation. A moisture meter can also be used to keep an eye on the habitat's humidity levels to make sure the right conditions are maintained for snail growth and reproduction.

Because snails need wet surroundings to grow, equipment like sprayers or misters is crucial for controlling humidity levels in the snail housing. For feeding, shallow trays or dishes work well for providing fresh greens and calcium supplements to snails. During normal care and harvesting, farmers should invest in protective gear such as gloves and boots to handle snails securely and hygienically. Ultimately, putting quality and functionality first guarantees effective administration and the expansion of the snail farm.

MAIN ADVANTAGES OF RAISING SNAILS

Several significant advantages make snail farming a desirable endeavor for both farmers and business owners. First of all, consumers can choose nutritious foods like snails because they are low in fat, high in protein, and full of vital elements like iron, calcium, and vitamins. In a world where concerns about food security and sustainability are growing, snails' nutritional profile presents them as a sustainable source of protein.

Second, those with limited land or resources can start snail farming on a modest scale and with little space requirements.

Snails are also hardy animals that can adjust to a wide range of environmental circumstances, which lowers the possibility of farming difficulties related to other livestock. Another benefit is their high rate of reproduction; in ideal circumstances, snails can produce hundreds of eggs a year, guaranteeing a consistent supply for trade. From an environmental point of view, snail farming encourages biodiversity by making use of areas that might not be appropriate for conventional cultivation. Because snails can consume organic matter and kitchen leftovers and turn them into important proteins, it also helps manage organic waste.

TYPICAL MYTHS AND FALSE BELIEFS REGARDING SNAIL FARMING

Notwithstanding its advantages, there are a lot of false beliefs and myths about snail farming that could put off prospective growers.

One widespread misconception is that raising snails is difficult and needs certain knowledge. In actuality, novices can establish and run a snail farm successfully with the right knowledge and assistance. There is also a myth that snails harm crops. A regulated setting is usually used to manage farmed snails, so they do not represent a hazard to crops, while certain wild snail species can be pests in gardens.

The idea that snails develop slowly and are not profitable is another fallacy. Snails are now a viable and profitable livestock choice because of advancements in breeding techniques and modern farming methods that have greatly increased their growth rates and reproductive effectiveness. Furthermore, there's a misperception that snail farming doesn't pay well. Conversely, snails can be sold as a gourmet food item and fetch high prices both domestically and abroad.

CHAPTER TWO

BEGINNING THE SNAIL FARMING PROCESS

SELECTING APPROPRIATE SNAIL SPECIES

Choosing the appropriate species of snails is essential for the success of any new snail farming endeavor. Due to their high rates of reproduction and ability to adapt to a variety of habitats, Helix aspersa, often known as the common garden snail, and Achatina fulica, sometimes known as the gigantic African snail, are popular candidates.

Achatina fulica grows better in warmer areas and is the favored species for larger-scale farming, although Helix aspersa is better suited for temperate climates and smaller-scale farming.

When selecting your snail species, keep things like market demand, local laws, and climate in mind. Helix aspersa grows well in controlled conditions, such as greenhouse setups or outdoor enclosures with sufficient shelter, and it enjoys moderate temperatures. Achatina fulica, on the other hand, thrives in areas with tropical or subtropical climates since it needs warmer temperatures and greater humidity levels. To choose the species of snail best suited to your particular farming objectives and environmental conditions, investigate local farming conditions and speak with knowledgeable snail farmers.

To ensure healthy stock and reduce the risk of illness or pest infestations, make sure the wholesalers or certified breeders you get your snails from are reliable. You can set up a sustainable and successful snail farming business by carefully choosing the appropriate species of snails based on your farming environment and objectives.

RECOGNIZING THE ENVIRONMENT AND SNAIL HABITATS

Since snails are environmentally sensitive, it's critical to comprehend what kind of habitat they need to successfully farm them. Conditions with high humidity, moderate temperatures, and lots of shade from the sun are ideal for snail growth. Shaded spaces that are well-ventilated and predator-free are ideal homes. For good growth and reproduction, whether you select indoor or outdoor farming, make sure the surroundings resemble their natural habitat.

Sustain constant humidity levels between 70 and 90 percent to avoid dehydration and guarantee sufficient moisture for the well-being of snails. Steer clear of places that flood easily or retain a lot of moisture, as these can cause fungal infections and respiratory problems in snails. Provide surfaces that allow for natural burrowing behavior while retaining moisture, such as dirt, peat moss, or coconut coir.

For your snails to live in a stable and comfortable environment, keep a close eye on temperature, humidity, and ventilation regularly. In your snail farming enterprise, you can maximize growth rates, reproductive success, and general health by comprehending and imitating the conditions of their natural habitat.

FUNDAMENTAL SNAIL ANATOMY AND PHYSIOLOGY

It's critical to comprehend the fundamental anatomy and physiology of snails to maintain and monitor their health on your farm. A muscular foot allows for locomotion and feeding, while a head contains sensory organs. Snails have a soft body covered in a hard shell. They use a radula, a device resembling a serrated tongue, to grind up vegetation and rasp food particles.

Despite having both male and female reproductive systems, snails are hermaphrodites and nevertheless need to mate to procreate.

Under ideal circumstances, they lay their eggs in clusters underground or in protected places, and the eggs hatch after a few weeks. Due to their sensitivity to environmental changes, snails require stable environments and a balanced diet to grow and thrive.

Understanding the anatomy and physiology of snails may help you recognize early warning indicators of health problems or possible problems, such as damage to the shell, unusual behavior, or abnormalities in reproduction. With this knowledge, you may optimize circumstances and put into practice the right care procedures to guarantee a successful snail farming endeavor.

ORGANIZING YOUR AREA FOR SNAIL FARMING

Establishing areas that are conducive to the best possible growth and reproduction is a necessary step in creating the ideal habitat for snail farming. In addition to taking ventilation, humidity, and temperature into account, picks a spot that has access to water and electricity, if necessary.

To shield snails from harsh weather and predators, outdoor farms should have covered spaces or buildings.

It is crucial to build housing units, such as pens or containers, with sufficient drainage and ventilation. Make use of sturdy, easily-cleanable materials like plastic, wood, or galvanized iron.

For burrowing and egg laying, provide substrates like dirt or coconut coir, but make sure they are chemical- and contaminant-free.

Organize your farm so that feeding, mating, and egg-laying regions are marked out to make managing and monitoring snails easier. To stop escapes and shield snails from predators like birds or rodents, erect fencing or barriers.

To guarantee hygiene, appropriate ventilation, and structural integrity, farming facilities should undergo routine inspections and maintenance.

You may provide a favorable atmosphere that promotes healthy growth, reproduction, and overall productivity in your snail farming business by carefully and methodically setting up your space.

SAFEGUARDS AND SANITATION PROCEDURES FOR SNAIL FARMING

For your snail farming business to be successful and sustainable, you must uphold strict safety and hygiene requirements. To reduce the risk of contamination and contamination to your health when handling snails or cleaning farming equipment, wear the proper protective gear, such as gloves and masks. To stop diseases or parasites from entering your farm, put strong biosecurity measures in place.

Use mild disinfectants to clean farming equipment, containers, and housing units regularly to get rid of diseases and keep the environment tidy for snails. Pesticides and chemicals should not be used close to snail habitats as this could endanger the health of the snails and jeopardize the safety of the product.

Maintain proper hygiene by carefully cleaning your hands both before and after touching farm equipment or snails. Maintain farming sites tidy and free of waste, expired food, and debris that could draw pests or disease-carrying organisms. To stop the spread of disease, keep an eye out for any symptoms of illness or stress in snails and rapidly separate those that show them.

You may establish a safe and sustainable environment that promotes healthy snail growth, improves product quality, and guarantees long-term success in the business by placing a high priority on safety and cleanliness in your snail farming operations.

CHAPTER THREE

SETTING UP YOUR FARM FOR SNAILS

HOW TO PREPARE AND CHOOSE SOIL

An effective snail farm requires prepared soil. Choose a place with loamy or sandy-loamy soil first, as these varieties allow for simple burrowing by snails and provide good drainage. Steer clear of clay soils, as they hold onto excess water and can suffocate snails. Remove any weeds, stones, and other debris from the area to prepare the soil. Next, till the soil to a depth of approximately 20 to 30 cm to guarantee that it is air-free and loose. Soil fertility and structure can be enhanced by adding organic matter, such as compost or well-rotted manure, which will make the soil more suitable for snail farming.

Check the pH of the soil after it has been prepared. Soils with a pH of 5.5 to 7.5 are ideal for snail growth and are slightly acidic to neutral. Soil pH is important for snail health because it impacts how well snails absorb calcium, which is necessary for shell growth. If your soil is too acidic, add agricultural lime to increase the pH. If your soil is too alkaline, apply sulfur to lower the pH. It is also important to keep the soil damp but not soggy to replicate the natural environment of snails.

Lastly, take into account the humidity and temperature of the soil. A temperature range of 25–30°C and a humidity content of 75–95% are ideal for snails. To help keep the soil evenly heated and hydrated, use cover crops or mulch. Keep an eye on these circumstances and modify them as needed. An effective snail farm starts with well-prepared and chosen soil, which creates the ideal conditions for development and reproduction.

BUILDING SNAIL HIDES AND PENS

Building appropriate snail enclosures and shelters is crucial to keeping snails safe from inclement weather and predators. Starting with a spot with some partial shadow is a good idea because direct sunshine can be harmful to snails. Make sure the pens you construct are well-ventilated by utilizing materials like concrete blocks, wire mesh, or wood. To keep predators out and to stop snails from escaping, the pens need to be at least 1.5 meters high. Installing a sturdy lid or cover is also essential to shield the snails from predators like birds.

Make the environment within the pens cozy and natural. This includes creating hiding places for snails to rest, such as turned-over clay pots, wooden planks, or mounds of organic material.

It is important to space out the shelters appropriately so that no snail feels crowded and can't find a place to hide. To keep the snails moist and give them a smooth surface to walk on, the pen's floor can be coated with a layer of leaves or organic materials.

Pen upkeep regularly is essential. Every week, clean the pens to get rid of any food scraps or garbage that could attract pests and spread illness. Water the soil frequently to keep it moist, but don't water it too much as this can promote the growth of fungi. Building and maintaining well-planned snail cages and shelters gives your snails a safe, cozy space that encourages healthy growth and reduces stress.

SELECTING MEAL PLANS AND FEEDING TECHNIQUES

Your snails' growth and well-being depend on the diet and feeding strategies you choose. As herbivores, snails do best when fed fruits, tubers, and green leafy vegetables. Carrots, sweet potatoes, cabbage, lettuce, and spinach are examples of common foods. Give them a balanced diet by adding calcium-rich foods like powdered limestone or crushed eggshells, which are essential for the development of shells.

The type of feeding you use will depend on how big your snail farm is. It makes sense to hand-feed on small farms. Just set the food items in shallow feeding trays or on the soil's surface. Automated feeding systems can be utilized on larger farms to minimize labor costs and distribute food uniformly. Whichever way you choose, be sure the food is clean and free of toxins and pesticides. To stop bacteria and mold from growing, remove any uneaten food every day.

Since snails are most active in the evening and early morning, it's crucial to set up a consistent feeding schedule. To avoid wastage and make sure every snail gets plenty to eat, keep an eye on the snails' feeding patterns and modify the amount of food as necessary. A diversified and nutrient-rich diet promotes the snails' general health and illness resistance in addition to facilitating their growth and reproduction.

WATERING SNAIL SYSTEMS

Water is essential to snail health since it helps with digestion, hydration, and general well-being. A well-designed watering system will guarantee that your snails get just the correct amount of moisture. Placing trays or shallow water dishes within the enclosures and making sure the snails can easily reach them are simple techniques. To stop bacteria and algae growth, regularly clean and refill these dishes with fresh, clean water.

Automated misting systems can be used for bigger snail farms. These devices create a thin mist that covers the pens, mimicking dew from nature and maintaining humidity without soaking the soil. To keep the pens at the ideal humidity levels, timers can be programmed to mist them in the morning or late at night. This technique saves work and guarantees a steady supply of moisture—a vital component for the health of snails.

Regularly checking the humidity levels is crucial, regardless of the method used for watering. Conditions between 75 and 95 percent humidity are ideal for snail growth. Dehydration can result from low humidity, while fungal infections can arise from high humidity. Measure the humidity with hygrometers and modify the frequency of watering as necessary. It is possible to establish an atmosphere that meets the physiological needs of snails and encourages healthy growth by keeping the moisture balance just right.

CONTROL TECHNIQUES FOR PREDATORS AND PESTS

Keeping your snail population healthy requires keeping pests and predators away from your snail farm. Birds, rodents, and insects like beetles and ants are common predators. Use strong materials and tight covers while building your pens to protect them from these dangers. Make sure the pen constructions are sturdy enough to discourage larger animals like rodents and install fine mesh or netting around the enclosures to keep out small predators.

Think about using biological control techniques in addition to physical barriers. Introduce frogs or specific bird species, which are natural predators of dangerous insects and can help control pest numbers. Check your snail pens frequently for indications of infestation, such as broken snail shells or holes in the ground. Quick action, such as hand-removing pests or using safe, organic insect repellents, is made possible by early discovery.

Keeping the snail farm hygienic and clean is also essential for controlling pests. Eliminate leftover food and rubbish as soon as possible to keep pests away. Keep the area around the pens clear of any trash and overgrown foliage so that bugs have nowhere to hide. A healthy and growing snail population can be ensured by protecting your snail farm from pests and predators through the use of physical barriers, preventive measures, and routine monitoring.

CHAPTER FOUR

CONTROLLING SNAIL PROCREATION

COMPREHENDING THE MATING BEHAVIOR OF SNAILS

Successful reproduction in snails depends on a fascinating and complex process called mating behavior. Since they have both male and female reproductive organs, snails are hermaphrodites, meaning that any two of them can mate. Snails participate in an hour-long wooing ritual before mating. To make sure they are compatible, they circle each other, touch tentacles, and exchange chemical signals. Farmers may create the perfect environment for mating by having a better understanding of this behavior.

Sustaining a favorable habitat is essential for mating. For mating behavior to be stimulated, snails need a soft substrate or soil that is well-hydrated and humid. Farmers need to keep an eye on the humidity and temperature to make sure it is similar to the snails' native environment.

By offering flora and hiding spots, you can also promote natural behaviors in snails, which increases their comfort level and likelihood of mating.

An indicator of a snail's health and reproductive readiness can be seen in its mating activity. While stressed or diseased snails may not participate in mating behaviors, healthy snails will. Through the identification of these behaviors and upholding ideal conditions, farmers may efficiently control snail reproduction and increase agricultural productivity.

PROCEDURES FOR LAYING AND INCUBATING EGGS

A crucial stage in the farming of snails is the laying of eggs by the successful mating of snails. Usually, where they can readily bury them, damp, loose dirt or substrate is where snails deposit their eggs. Depending on the species and surroundings, a single snail can lay anywhere from 50 to 100 eggs at a time. To ensure that the soil in the breeding region stays moist and undisturbed, farmers should routinely check it for egg clusters.

Snail egg incubation demands close monitoring of humidity and temperature. 20–25°C is the ideal temperature range for incubation, and 80–90% humidity is ideal as well. To retain moisture, farmers can accomplish these conditions by applying a thin layer of organic material, such as leaves, to the soil. Water logging the soil must be avoided as this might cause egg rot and lower hatching success.

Gently examining the egg clusters regularly without upsetting them too much is part of monitoring the incubation process. Depending on the species, the eggs will hatch into baby snails after two to three weeks. Maintaining optimal incubation conditions increases hatch rates and helps the farm's snail population grow.

TAKING CARE OF YOUNG SNAILS AND HATCHLINGS

To ensure their survival and growth, the tiny hatchlings need special care once the eggs hatch. Because of their great fragility, hatchlings are susceptible to environmental changes, predators, and dehydration. To assist the hatchlings' early development, farmers should house them in a controlled environment that is similar to the incubation circumstances in terms of temperature and humidity.

Hatchling growth depends on feeding them. Soft, leafy greens and finely ground, calcium-rich food—like powdered cuttlebone—should be given to young snails. This diet promotes general health and shell growth. Overfeeding should be avoided, and any uneaten food should be removed to stop mold growth and contamination, which can be dangerous for young snails.

As the hatchlings get bigger, progressively moving them into more spacious enclosures and offering a greater range of food aids in their environmental adaptation. Maintaining ideal living conditions and keeping an eye out for any symptoms of disease or stress will guarantee that the young snails grow into healthy adults who are prepared for the following phases of their life cycle.

PHASES OF GROWTH AND DEVELOPMENT

A thorough understanding of the snails' life cycles and growth phases is necessary for efficient farming management. From hatchlings to adults, snails go through multiple growth stages, each with its requirements for nutrition and environment.

Hatchlings are tiny and delicate at first, needing high humidity and food strong in calcium to help their quick development and shell creation.

Snails become more robust and active as they mature into the juvenile stage. They need extra room during this stage, as well as a varied diet rich in veggies, leafy greens, and calcium supplements.

To make sure the animals get enough nutrients, farmers should keep an eye on their growth rate and modify their feeding techniques. A healthy habitat can be maintained by giving them new food and water regularly and by cleaning their habitat.

The mature snail reaches its peak development and is prepared for reproduction. At this stage, it's critical to divide them according to age and size to avoid congestion and resource rivalry. Sustaining a constant reproductive cycle and a sustainable snail population on the farm requires maintaining ideal conditions for adult snails, such as appropriate mating habitats and sufficient nutrients.

BREEDING STRATEGIES TO BOOST YIELD

Using efficient breeding methods is essential to raising the productivity of snail farming. Farmers can use a method called selective breeding, in which they pick the healthiest and most productive snails to reproduce. Farmers can improve the general quality and production of their snail population by carefully choosing mating partners based on factors such as size, health, and reproductive success.

Increased yield can also be attributed to well-managed breeding conditions. Snails mate more frequently when breeding pens are provided with perfect conditions, including high humidity, ideal temperature, and an ample supply of food. Keeping these habitats free from intruders and predators increases the likelihood of successful fertilization and egg-laying.

Rotational breeding techniques are another tool that farmers can use to keep a steady cycle of production. Farmers can guarantee a year-round supply of eggs and hatchlings by separating the snail population into breeding groups and alternating them between breeding and resting phases. Maintaining a balanced and healthy snail population minimizes stress on the snails, helps prevent overbreeding, and maximizes production.

CHAPTER FIVE

MANAGEMENT OF HEALTH AND DISEASE

COMMON SNAIL ILLNESSES AND PARASITES

Similar to other animals, snails are prone to a range of illnesses and parasites. These can include bacterial illnesses, fungal infections, and parasitic infestations like nematodes and mites. While bacterial diseases can cause the snail to generate excessive mucus, appear lethargic, or develop shell rot, fungal infections typically show up as white or grey spots on the snail's body or shell. In contrast, parasitic infestations are typically recognized by the presence of microscopic, moving creatures inside the substrate or on the snail's body. Maintaining a healthy snail farm requires an understanding of these frequent ailments.

A balanced feed, regular hygiene and humidity control are just a few examples of good farm management techniques that can dramatically lower the incidence of chronic illnesses.

It's crucial to often check snail habitats for indications of disease or infestation. Disease transmission can be stopped and losses can be reduced with early detection and prompt response. Maintaining a farm environment that is both healthy and supportive of snail growth requires the implementation of a regular sanitation program that includes cleaning housing and equipment.

To prevent the spread of disease, fresh snails should be isolated before being added to the main population. Infections can also be stopped from spreading quickly by making sure snail populations are not overloaded. To maintain a healthy and successful snail farm, farmers should be aware of the common illnesses and parasites that afflict snails and take proactive measures to manage them.

SIGNS AND PROMPT METHODS OF IDENTIFICATION

Early detection of disease symptoms in snails can prevent serious losses for your farm. Behavior changes like decreased activity, decreased hunger, and increased mucus production are common symptoms.

Health problems can also be indicated by physical symptoms such as discoloration, swelling, and abnormal growths on the body or shell. Regularly keeping an eye out for these indications in snails is essential for early detection.

Snails should be examined individually regularly to check for any indications of disease or suffering. Observing their feeding habits and mobility during regular feeding times is a straightforward yet effective technique.

While sick snails may be lethargic and exhibit little interest in food, healthy snails are often lively and feed easily. It is also crucial to check the snail's shell for any damage or abnormalities, as the shell can frequently reveal information about the health of the snail as a whole.

Keeping an eye on the farm's environmental circumstances is another early detection technique. To stop disease breakouts, make sure that cleanliness, temperature, and humidity are all kept at ideal levels.

Snails can be examined closely using a magnifying glass to assist find micro parasites that may not be visible to the unaided eye. Maintaining thorough documentation of each snail's condition and any treatments given might make it easier to monitor and control health problems.

EFFECTIVE PREVENTION AND TREATMENT TECHNIQUES

Treatment must begin as soon as a disease or parasite infestation is identified to stop it from spreading. Medicated baths are occasionally used in conjunction with antifungal or antibacterial medications, although specific treatments depend on the ailment or parasite type. Applying a diluted antifungal solution directly to the afflicted region can help treat fungal infections. Antibiotics for bacterial illnesses might be necessary; to guarantee proper dosages and efficacy, these drugs should be given by veterinary advice.

Preventive measures, such as maintaining ideal environmental conditions and appropriate diet, are equally vital.

Equipment and housing for snails should be cleaned and disinfected regularly to assist avoid the growth of pathogens. Providing snails with a well-rounded diet that is high in calcium and other vital nutrients strengthens their immune system and aids in disease prevention. Establishing a routine for health monitoring aids in the early identification of possible problems before they spread widely.

Utilizing biological controls, such as beneficial insects that feed on snail parasites, is another successful preventive tactic. Furthermore, breaking the life cycle of numerous parasites can be achieved by turning snail cages and letting the soil rest. To keep ahead of any health problems, farmers should also educate themselves on the newest methods for raising snails and disease control strategies.

PROCEDURES FOR SICK SNAILS IN QUARANTINE

One of the most important measures in stopping the spread of illness within a snail farm is to quarantine sick snails. A sick snail should be separated from the healthy colony as soon as possible. This entails transferring the sick snail to an area that is clean, isolated, and devoid of other snails. Equipping the quarantine section with the same environmental controls—such as appropriate humidity and temperature levels—as the main farm is crucial.

The snail should be closely observed for any changes in symptoms and general health during the quarantine period. During this time, particular therapies can be given without endangering the well-being of the snail population as a whole. To stop more infections, it's critical to keep the quarantine environment clean and hygienic. The disease can be contained by routinely cleaning the quarantine enclosure and handling sick snails with disposable gloves.

In addition, before releasing the snail to the main population, quarantine protocols entail watching it for a predetermined amount of time—typically two to four weeks—to make sure it has fully recovered. If more than one snail is afflicted, they ought to be kept apart from the healthy snails but in quarantine together. More effective management and prevention of future outbreaks can be achieved by keeping thorough records of the snails in quarantine, including the treatments used and the progress noted.

VETERINARY ADVICE AND TREATMENT

Maintaining a healthy population of snails can be greatly aided by consulting with a veterinarian who has experience with snail farming.

Veterinarians are qualified to diagnose conditions accurately, suggest appropriate courses of action for managing and preventing illness, and provide advice on best practices. Even in cases where there are no obvious health concerns, routine veterinary examinations can help detect possible abnormalities before they worsen.

Regular health examinations, immunizations (if available), and guidance on diet and environmental management should all be part of veterinary care.

Veterinarians can perform laboratory testing to determine the precise pathogen and suggest targeted therapies in cases of illness outbreaks. To guarantee therapy efficacy and safety, they can also offer advice on how to administer and dose medications correctly.

Developing a relationship with a veterinarian can also offer continuing assistance and instruction on managing the health of snails. They can provide farmers with information on newly discovered illnesses, potential dangers, and improvements in available therapies. Snail farmers may make sure their farming methods are current and their snails stay healthy and productive by routinely checking with a veterinarian.

CHAPTER SIX

GATHERING AND HANDLING SNAILS

ASSESSING THE MATURITY OF SNAILS FOR HARVESTING

Determining the snails' maturity is essential for ensuring the best possible harvest yields and quality. Maturity for snails usually occurs between six and twelve months, depending on the species and surroundings. Size and physical traits are useful in identifying mature snails. Depending on the species, they should have a smooth, completely grown shell with a diameter of two to three inches. The thickness of the shell, which gets firmer as the snail ages, is another clue. Mature snails also move more actively and are less likely to become stressed.

Examine your snail population regularly to determine snail maturity accurately. Size-wise group the snails and keep an eye on their habits and shell quality. Small or delicately shelled snails should be given more time to mature as they are not yet mature. For your snail farm to remain sustainable and to produce as much as possible, your snails must be fully matured. You can maximize the output and quality of your snail produce by harvesting at the right time by knowing the signs of maturity.

HUMANE AND ETHICAL HARVESTING METHODS

To protect the well-being of the snails and preserve the quality of the product, ethical and humane harvesting techniques are essential in snail farming. It's important to treat snails gently when harvesting them to reduce stress and protect their shells. Without hurting the snails, carefully remove them from their surroundings using specialized instruments like tweezers or tiny tongs. Steer clear of harsh treatment or using too much force on the snails as this can be detrimental to their wellbeing.

After harvesting, keep the snails moist and avoid suffocating by transferring them in well-ventilated containers. Steer clear of crowded areas when being transported to minimize strain and guarantee sufficient ventilation.

After harvesting, keep snails cool and shady to avoid drying out and scorching. Provide snails with a comfortable environment that is the right temperature and humidity until they are processed further or sold.

Sustainable snail farming is encouraged by ethical harvesting methods, which also improve the quality of snail output. You support an ethical and compassionate approach to farming techniques by putting your snails' welfare first during the harvesting process.

SNAILS BEING CLEANED AND READY FOR THE MARKET

An essential stage in guaranteeing the hygienic conditions and superior quality of the finished product is cleaning and preparing snails for sale. To begin, properly wash the gathered snails in clean water to get rid of any dirt, debris, or slime residue. Take care not to harm the snails' fragile skin as you gently scrub their bodies and shells with a gentle brush or sponge. To make sure that all impurities are gone, rinse the snails several times until the water runs clear.

Once cleaned, rid snails of any leftover contaminants or unwanted flavors before putting them on the market. Snails should be kept in a clean container with fresh water and fed either commercial snail feed or fresh vegetables for a period of two to three days. The meat from the snails is cleaner and more appetizing as a result of this process, which helps clear their digestive tracts.

After being purified, give the snails another rinse and check their quality and preparedness. If any snails exhibit symptoms of disease or injury, remove them to preserve the integrity of the product.

To promote airflow and avoid suffocation, place cleaned snails in breathable containers like mesh bags or perforated boxes. Before putting packed snails up for sale or undergoing additional processing, keep them in a cool, humid place to maintain their freshness.

METHODS OF PROCESSING FOR VARIOUS PRODUCTS

To satisfy consumer tastes and market expectations, multiple methods must be used while processing snails into different items. Snail meat in a can is a popular product that is produced by cleaning and cooking snails until they are soft. Snails should be boiled, then taken out of their shells, completely cleaned, and placed in cans with oil or brine to preserve them. Cans should be properly sealed to preserve freshness and extend shelf life.

Snails are cleaned, blanched, and then removed from their shells in hot water for another processing method called freezing snail meat. To avoid freezer burn and preserve quality, freeze snail meat in appropriate freezer-safe containers or vacuum-seal bags. Snail meat that has been frozen for a long time can be utilized in a variety of recipes, including sautés, stews, and soups.

As needed, clean and prepare snails, making sure they are thoroughly cleaned and purged to obtain fresh snail flesh. To preserve freshness and avoid spoiling, keep fresh snail flesh refrigerated. Put fresh snails in vacuum-sealed bags or airtight containers before distributing them to markets and restaurants or selling them at retail.

You may efficiently serve to various market niches and diversify your snail goods by utilizing suitable processing procedures. Optimizing the value and profitability of your snail farming endeavor can be achieved by comprehending the preferences of your target market and modifying your processing techniques accordingly.

GUIDELINES FOR PACKAGING AND STORING

To preserve product quality and guarantee client satisfaction, packaging and storage are essential components of snail farming. After processing, place snails in hygienic, ventilated containers to avoid moisture buildup and to allow for air circulation. Steer clear of airtight packing, which can swiftly decompose or suffocate snails.

To help with traceability and to inform consumers, labels on packaged snails should include important information such as the species type, harvest date, and storage directions. Appropriate labeling guarantees regulatory compliance and fosters customer trust.

To maintain freshness and avoid dehydration, store packed snails in a cool, humid place. Temperatures of 10-15°C (50-59°F) and high humidity levels of 70-90% are ideal for storage. Regularly check storage conditions to avoid temperature swings and guarantee the best possible quality for your goods.

You can preserve the quality and shelf life of your snail goods and make sure they reach customers in the best possible condition by adhering to these packing and storing requirements. Snail farming businesses can improve their reputation and increase client satisfaction by implementing efficient packaging and storage techniques.

CHAPTER SEVEN

HOW TO PROMOTE AND SELL YOUR SNAILS

CHOOSING THE MARKET YOU WANT TO ENTER

For your snail farming endeavor to be successful, determining your target market is essential. Start by looking into the demographics that are most likely to be interested in snail items, such as age, gender, geography, and economic level. Take into account variables that affect the consumption of snails, such as cultural customs, health-conscious consumers, and culinary preferences. To learn more about the tastes and purchase patterns of potential clients, conduct surveys or market research. You may effectively adapt your marketing efforts and product offerings by having a thorough understanding of your target market.

After determining who your target market is, concentrate on developing an extensive client profile. Your prospective clientele's particular traits and preferences ought to be included in this profile.

For instance, if your products appeal to health-conscious people, emphasize the nutritional value and organic quality of your snails. Use online discussion boards, social media sites, and neighborhood get-togethers to interact with and obtain input from your target market.

You can better suit the demands and preferences of your target market by modifying your agricultural techniques and marketing strategies as you get a deeper understanding of them.

BUILDING A NAME FOR YOUR PRODUCTS MADE FROM SNAILS

Establishing a robust brand for your snail goods helps you stand out in the crowded agricultural product industry. Create a unique selling proposition (USP) outlining what sets your snail goods apart from the competition first. This could involve organic certification, sustainable farming methods, or distinctive flavor qualities. Create a packaging and a distinctive brand logo that accurately represents the standards and principles of your snail farm. To increase consumer identification and trust in your brand, make sure your branding is consistent across all platforms and marketing materials.

Create a captivating brand narrative that appeals to your target market next. Tell the story of your snail farm, highlighting things like family customs, community service, and ethical farming methods. Using storytelling in your marketing can help you stand out from the competition and establish an emotional connection with your target audience. To promote your snail goods and expand your audience, work with influencers or professionals in the culinary or health sectors. By making branding and narrative investments, you can create a devoted clientele that appreciates your goods and helps your snail farming enterprise.

PROFITABILITY-DRIVEN PRICING STRATEGIES

The key to increasing profitability in snail farming is creating efficient pricing methods. To start, figure out all the expenditures related to producing snails, including labor, feed, housing, and administrative fees, by performing a comprehensive cost analysis. When determining your rates, take into account consumer demand and market prices to make sure they are both profitable and competitive.

To appeal to diverse client categories and boost sales volume, think about providing several pricing levels or bundles.

To maximize revenue, use dynamic pricing techniques based on market trends or seasonal demand. For instance, you might marginally raise pricing to take advantage of spikes in demand during periods of high snail consumption or on holidays. To stay competitive in the market, keep an eye on your rivals' pricing tactics and modify your own accordingly.

Explain the worth of your snail goods to support your price and draw attention to their high quality, nutritive content or environmentally friendly farming methods. Keep an eye on your pricing tactics and make necessary adjustments in response to consumer feedback and market conditions to keep your snail farming business profitable and growing.

NETWORKS OF DISTRIBUTION AND SALES CHANNELS

To reach your target market and increase sales of your snail goods, you must select the appropriate sales channels and distribution networks. Consider the tastes and purchasing patterns of your target market when evaluating online and offline sales channels. To promote and sell your snail products, form alliances with nearby restaurants, specialty food shops, farmers' markets, and grocery stores.

Make use of social media and e-commerce platforms to expand your audience and provide online sales and home delivery choices.

Create a strong distribution network to guarantee that clients receive fresh snail items on time. To preserve product quality throughout transit, take into account logistics considerations including chilled transportation and packaging. Use effective inventory control procedures to prevent stockouts and quickly complete customer orders. To improve operations and increase your market reach, cultivate a solid rapport with retailers, distributors, and logistical partners.

Keep an eye out for opportunities to optimize performance and satisfy the changing needs of your snail farming business by regularly monitoring your sales channels and distribution networks.

RELATIONSHIP MANAGEMENT WITH CUSTOMERS

To cultivate repeat business and loyalty in your snail farming enterprise, you must use effective customer relationship management (CRM). Establishing clear routes of contact for questions, comments, and help from customers should come first.

Answer consumer questions as soon as possible, and handle any problems or complaints professionally and sympathetically. Establish a strategy for collecting feedback from customers to learn more about their satisfaction levels and pinpoint areas where your goods and services need to be improved.

Offer customized specials, loyalty programs, or recommendations to customers based on their past purchases and personal preferences to personalize your interactions with them.

 Communicate with clients via blogs, email newsletters, and social media to inform them of farm updates and to explain the advantages of purchasing snail goods.

To segment your audience and target marketing initiatives at particular client groups, gather and evaluate consumer data.

To increase your company's legitimacy and social evidence, solicit client endorsements and reviews.

You can build enduring relationships with consumers, promote word-of-mouth recommendations, and set your innovative goods apart in the crowded market by giving customer relationship management priority.

Maintaining consistent growth and profitability for your snail farming company requires you to constantly assess and improve your CRM strategy in response to shifting consumer preferences and market conditions.

CHAPTER EIGHT

REGULATORY AND LEGAL ASPECTS

LICENSES & PERMITS FOR SNAIL FARMING

To legally function, starting a snail farming business requires obtaining the required licenses and permits. The first step is to find out which particular licenses are needed in your area by contacting the local environmental and agricultural authorities. This often entails land use permission if your farm is located in an area classified as rural or semi-urban, a normal business license, and a special permit for animal farming. Making sure you have all of these licenses helps you prevent potential fines and shutdowns in addition to keeping your business operating legally.

The next step is to get the necessary paperwork ready if you are aware of the permits that are needed. Environmental impact evaluations, documentation of land ownership or lease, and a thorough business plan are a few examples of this.

In certain situations, you might additionally have to provide proof that you possess the required knowledge or have completed snail farming training. It can take some time to gather and arrange these documents, so start early and be thorough to prevent delays.

The last step is to send your application to the relevant authorities. Be ready for site inspections, when representatives will verify that your establishments adhere to all applicable environmental, health, and safety regulations. Several weeks to months may pass during this process, depending on your location and the intricacy of your farm. Maintain contact with the authorities to guarantee a seamless approval procedure, and act quickly to resolve any concerns they point out.

OBSERVANCE OF SAFETY AND HEALTH REGULATIONS

For snail farming to be successful, health and safety regulations must be followed. First and foremost, producers need to follow regulations to establish a secure and hygienic environment for workers and snails alike. This entails utilizing safe and authorized materials for snail housing, adhering to regular cleaning schedules, and maintaining good cleanliness. Staff members can avoid illness and infection by receiving training on proper cleanliness and handling techniques, which will keep the snails healthy and productive.

Processes and packaging related to snails are likewise subject to health regulations. From harvest to sale, farmers must adhere to certain procedures to guarantee that snails are handled safely and cleanly. This could entail following labeling and packaging specifications, keeping cold storage facilities up to date, and employing stainless steel equipment. Maintaining thorough documentation of these procedures might be beneficial during audits and inspections.

Worker safety regulations are just as crucial. Employees are shielded from potential risks by ensuring that all farm operations adhere to occupational health and safety regulations. This includes supplying personal protective equipment (PPE), making certain that chemicals are handled safely, and keeping machinery in excellent operating condition. Workers can maintain awareness of safety procedures and learn how to handle emergencies by participating in regular training and drills.

IMPACT ASSESSMENTS AND ENVIRONMENTAL REGULATIONS

Environmental restrictions are important in snail farming since inappropriate methods might damage the ecosystem in the area. An environmental impact assessment (EIA) is a requirement for farmers to determine any possible adverse consequences of their farming operations. This evaluation looks at things like waste management, water and land use, and the effect on the surrounding wildlife and vegetation. The findings help farmers adopt environmentally friendly techniques that reduce their impact on the environment.

An essential component of compliance is efficient waste management. Organic waste from snail farms needs to be managed carefully to avoid pollution.

Snail waste can be composted to produce beneficial fertilizer and lessen its impact on the environment. In addition, farmers ought to put in place buffer zones of vegetation and appropriate drainage systems to stop runoff and soil erosion.

The utilization of resources like land and water is another crucial aspect. The farm's environmental impact can be decreased by implementing sustainable water management techniques, such as rainwater harvesting systems and recycling water in snail cages. Furthermore, it's critical to choose territory that can support snail farming without negatively affecting nearby ecosystems. By adhering to these rules, snail farming can continue to be sustainable and environmentally friendly.

PROTECTION OF INTELLECTUAL PROPERTY FOR INNOVATIONS

New equipment designs, feeding formulae, or breeding strategies are examples of innovations in snail farming that might be important assets that need to be protected.

Patents, trademarks, and copyrights are examples of intellectual property (IP) rights that aid in securing these breakthroughs and preventing unapproved use. For example, getting a patent can prevent competitors from copying your invention if you create a novel snail-feed formula.

The first step in protecting intellectual property is to fully document your inventions. Detailed documentation that includes test findings, prototypes, and diagrams will help your intellectual property applications. To find out the appropriate kind of protection for your invention, speak with an intellectual property lawyer. They may help you with the application procedure, which could include presenting technical specifications, evidence of commercial feasibility, and proof of originality.

You must remain vigilant to protect your intellectual property. Keep an eye out for any possible violations in the market, and be ready to take legal action to defend your rights if needed.

A cash stream can also be generated by licensing agreements, which let others utilize your inventions while you keep ownership. Snail farmers may safeguard their investments and promote continued innovation in the sector by obtaining and managing intellectual property rights.

REQUIREMENTS FOR BUSINESS REGISTRATION AND TAXATION

For legal compliance and financial management, you must register your snail farming firm and comprehend the associated taxation obligations. Start by registering your company with the relevant national and local agencies. Choosing a business structure (such as a corporation, partnership, or sole proprietorship), registering a business name, and requesting a tax identification number (TIN) are usually steps in this procedure.

Maintaining precise financial records and becoming up to date on applicable taxes are essential to comprehending the tax responsibilities associated with snail farming. This covers sales tax, income tax, and maybe other taxes or subsidies unique to agriculture. To make sure you are aware of all the credits and deductions available to agricultural enterprises, speak with a tax advisor. They can assist you in creating a tax plan that ensures compliance and optimizes benefits.

To prevent fines and interest, it is essential to file tax returns regularly and pay any taxes owed on time. Establish a reliable accounting system to keep track of all your earnings, outlays, and tax-related paperwork. Accounting software can make this process easier and assist in producing the required financial reports. Maintaining a proactive and systematic approach to tax administration can guarantee that your snail farming enterprise runs effectively and stays in good standing with the tax authorities.

CHAPTER NINE

GROWING YOUR SNAIL FARMING ENTERPRISE

BOOSTING THE CAPACITY OF PRODUCTION

The first step in increasing snail farming production capacity is to maximize your current infrastructure and resources. Start by evaluating the space, tools, and resources that are currently accessible for your farming setup. Enhance the productivity of your farming activities by keeping the snail pens clean and well-maintained and by putting good feeding and breeding plans in place. You can increase your capacity by adding more snail pens or by making your current ones larger. Make use of sophisticated breeding methods, like selective breeding, to boost your snails' quality and rate of reproduction.

Investing in technology and automation can increase production capacity even more. An ideal environment for snail growth can be created with automated feeding systems, temperature control, and humidity regulation, which will decrease the amount of manual effort needed and increase efficiency.

Using data monitoring devices to keep tabs on your snails' growth and well-being will help you spot problems early and take swift action. You may reduce resource waste and increase productivity by utilizing technology.

Additionally, think about increasing the actual area of your farm. If your present location permits, purchase nearby land to expand the space set aside for snail farming.

As an alternative, think about establishing more farming sites in climates that are appropriate. Working together with other farmers can also be a successful tactic, as you can pool resources and expertise to boost output as a group. You can maintain efficiency and growth in your farming operations by routinely evaluating and improving them.

RECRUITING AND OUTSOURCING SUPPORT

Hiring help and outsourcing are essential elements to successfully growing your snail farming company. Determine which responsibilities, such as marketing, sales, and logistics, can be outsourced first. Hiring professionals in these areas will free you up to concentrate on your primary farming duties.

You may find experts who specialize in these fields through platforms like Up work or Freelancer, and they can offer high-quality services without requiring full-time staff. Moreover, operations can be streamlined by outsourcing administrative work, giving you more time to concentrate on increasing output.

Employing help for tasks around the farm is equally crucial. Expert labor can boost output and guarantee the smooth operation of farming activities. Hire personnel with a background in farming, particularly in snail farming. Training courses can aid in a new hire's rapid assimilation into the norms and procedures of your farm.

Universities and local agricultural extension offices can be excellent sources of skilled workers. Efficient teamwork and seamless daily operations can be ensured by clearly defining roles and duties.

In addition to providing competitive pay and benefits, a positive work environment is essential to keeping staff on board and developing a solid support network. To maintain the motivation and engagement of your workforce, offer possibilities for professional progression and ongoing education. Keep a close eye on the performance of both your internal and external personnel, and make necessary adjustments to ensure that high standards of efficiency and productivity are maintained. Your snail farming company can develop and succeed significantly with a well-organized crew.

SYSTEMS FOR MANAGING INVENTORY EFFECTIVELY

A strong inventory management system must be put in place if you want to grow your snail farming company. Make a list of every asset, such as farming equipment, feed, and breeding stock, to start. Utilize digital technologies for managing your inventory to stay up to date on your resources instantly. To make sure you never run out of necessary supplies, these technologies can assist estimate demand, keeping an eye on stock levels, and automating reordering procedures. Precise inventory management reduces waste and optimizes the use of resources.

It's also critical to establish precise procedures for managing and storing goods. To prevent misunderstanding, assign distinct spaces for various inventory kinds and put labeling procedures in place. Frequent inventory audits and inspections will assist in spotting irregularities early and averting losses. Accuracy and consistency in the use of resources are ensured by teaching your employees on good inventory management techniques. A well-maintained inventory system keeps your farm running smoothly and minimizes downtime.

Moreover, operations can be streamlined by linking your inventory management system with other company procedures like sales and procurement. Customer satisfaction can be increased by, for instance, automatically updating stock availability through the integration of inventory data with your sales platform. Your inventory system's data can also help you make more informed purchases by allowing you to modify orders in response to seasonal demand or buy in bulk when needed.

Maintaining operational effectiveness and fostering business growth is contingent upon proficient inventory management.

BUDGETING AND FINANCIAL PLANNING

Budgeting and financial planning are essential for growing your snail farming company. Make a thorough budget at first, listing all of your predicted spending together with your income. Add in expenses for labor, feed, equipment, marketing, and unforeseen costs.

Track your spending and income with financial management software to get up-to-date information about your financial situation. Update your budget regularly to account for shifts in the market and how your company operates.

Setting definite financial objectives and benchmarks is a necessary step in creating a financial strategy. Establish both short- and long-term goals, such as growing your production or breaking into new markets.

Invest money wisely on projects that will spur expansion, such as marketing campaigns or technological advancements. It's crucial to keep your cash flow in check, so keep a careful eye on your accounts payable and receivable to make sure payments are made on schedule. Maintaining financial stability and managing unforeseen expenses can be facilitated by having a contingency reserve.

To improve your financial plans, consult agricultural extension services or financial advisors. Examine your choices for financing, including grants, loans, and investment opportunities, to support your expansion goals. Producing thorough financial forecasts and reports will aid in luring in possible backers or obtaining capital.

You can make wise judgments and stay on track with your goals by doing regular financial evaluations. To keep your snail farming business growing and profitable, you must practice sound financial planning and budgeting.

STRATEGIES FOR EXPANSION AND UPCOMING GROWTH

Snail farming expansion tactics include product diversification, brand enhancement, and market exploration. Begin by investigating both domestic and foreign markets that might be interested in your items. Your expansion initiatives can be guided by having a thorough understanding of the demand, competition, and regulatory requirements in new markets. Creating a compelling marketing plan that emphasizes the features and advantages of your snail goods can draw in new clients and foster brand loyalty.

Another way to spur growth is to diversify your product line. Apart from vending consumable snails, contemplate creating goods derived from snails, like makeup, fertilizers, or pet food. You may boost profitability and create new revenue streams by adding value to your products.

To help direct your efforts in product development, conduct market research to find trends and customer preferences. Creating joint ventures or co-branding partnerships with other companies might help you expand your market and product offerings.

Both ongoing innovation and market adaptation are essential for future growth. Make research and development investments to advance sustainable practices, product quality, and farming methods. Keep up with developments in technology and industry trends that can improve your business.

Creating a powerful online presence on social media, e-commerce sites, and a business website can boost exposure and draw in more visitors. You can achieve long-term growth and success in your snail farming business by putting these expansion tactics into practice.

CHAPTER TEN

FAQS & TROUBLESHOOTING

TYPICAL OBSTACLES SNAIL FARMERS FACE

A venture's success may be impacted by a number of the obstacles that come with snail farming. Keeping snails in their ideal habitat is one of the most frequent problems. For them to flourish, a particular range of humidity and temperature is necessary. Snails risk becoming dormant or, worse, dying if these requirements are not fulfilled. This problem is most noticeable in areas with erratic weather. To maintain stable conditions, farmers must make investments in suitable housing and monitoring systems.

The management of pests and predators presents another major challenge. Ants, vermin, and birds are just a few of the many hazards that snails are vulnerable to. In the wrong hands, these predators can wipe out a snail population. To reduce these hazards, farmers must put preventative measures in place including safe enclosures and routine monitoring. Furthermore, illnesses can spread swiftly among snail populations, necessitating careful health supervision and perhaps quarantine procedures for young or ill snails.

Finally, snails can have complicated nutritional and feeding requirements. To grow robust shells, they need a diet high in calcium and well-balanced. However guaranteeing a steady supply of the appropriate feed can be challenging, particularly for inexperienced farmers. Setting up a dependable feeding schedule and being aware of the nutritional requirements are essential. It is possible to treat nutritional deficits and encourage healthy growth by feeding a varied diet that includes fruits, vegetables, and commercial feed.

SOLVING ISSUES WITH SNAIL FARMING

The first thing to do when faced with difficulties in snail farming is to pinpoint the precise problem that is harming the snails. Low reproduction rates, high mortality, and poor growth rates are typical issues. For example, if snails are not growing as they should, it can be because of poor environmental conditions or insufficient nutrients. Growth problems can be addressed by examining the feed's quality and diversity and making sure the habitat has the right humidity and temperature.

Elevated death rates frequently indicate more severe issues, such as illness outbreaks or predator attacks. It's crucial to get regular checkups and to keep an eye out for any symptoms of disease, such as unusual slime production or inactivity. It's crucial to isolate sick snails and see a veterinarian if disease is detected. Effective protection against predators can be achieved by fortifying enclosures and utilizing barriers or repellents.

Unsuitable mating settings, poor food, and stress can all contribute to reproductive problems. Breeding results can be enhanced by providing snails with enough space, healthy food, and a mating habitat. Stress levels are lowered and natural mating activities are encouraged when hiding places and a peaceful setting are provided.

Snail farming success rates can be greatly increased by taking quick, practical action to address these typical issues.

FAQS REGARDING METHODS OF SNAIL FARMING

One question that comes up a lot is "How to start a snail farm." Newcomers frequently enquire about the prerequisites and first setup. Choosing an appropriate species, setting up the habitat, and obtaining healthy snails are the first steps in starting a snail farm. It's critical to select a species that thrives in the climate where you live. The habitat should have enough soil, moisture, and shelter to resemble natural settings.

A frequently asked question relates to feeding procedures. Many times, novice farmers wonder what and how much to feed their snails. Fruits, greens, and calcium-rich diets are essential for snails. To make sure they always have food, it's advised to give them a combination of lettuce, cabbage, and commercial snail feed.

The health of the snails can be preserved by keeping an eye on their eating habits and modifying amounts according to their intake.

Regarding breeding and boosting snail populations, farmers also raise lots of questions. Setting up a mating habitat with the right temperature and humidity levels is necessary for effective breeding. Natural reproduction is encouraged when there are enough hiding places and the ecosystem is stress-free. Gradually, the population of snails can be increased by regularly searching for eggs and offering a haven for hatchlings.

PROFESSIONAL SUCCESS SUGGESTIONS AND GUIDANCE

Careful planning and ongoing education are frequently essential for success in snail farming. One important piece of advice is to start small and grow over time. With this strategy, novice farmers can grow and adjust without having to worry about suffering large losses. A strong foundation for future expansion is created by starting with a modest number of snails and concentrating on fine-tuning the environment and feeding schedules.

Investing in quality rather than quantity is another important piece of advice. Although they may initially cost more, high-quality snails and feed produce greater results over the long run. In addition to growing more quickly and reproducing more successfully, healthy snails also resist illness. Similar to this, purchasing appropriate housing and environmental controls guarantees ideal circumstances for raising snails.

Joining pertinent agricultural associations and establishing connections with seasoned snail growers offer priceless help and insights. New farmers can avoid frequent problems by learning from the experiences of more seasoned farmers and receiving helpful advice. Farmers can stay informed about new developments in snail farming and best practices by attending workshops, taking courses, and reading current publications.

COMMUNITY RESOURCES AND ASSISTANCE

A snail farming endeavor can be substantially improved by utilizing community assistance. Joining online or local agricultural groups gives you access to a plethora of information and experiences that people have shared. These groups frequently provide guidance, solve issues, and share success stories that can motivate and assist beginning farmers. Taking part in local agricultural activities and participating in forums can facilitate the development of a peer support network.

It might also be helpful to have access to resources like government programs, agricultural experts, and extension services. Agricultural extension services are available in many areas and provide farmers with resources, training, and guidance at no cost or a reduced cost. These services can offer information on business prospects, pest control techniques, and best practices.

By using learning tools like books, webinars, and online courses, farmers can keep up with the most recent advancements in snail farming.

Numerous academic institutions and agricultural associations provide cost-effective or complimentary resources that address different facets of snail farming. Farmers are better able to adjust to obstacles and seize new possibilities when they maintain a connection with the farming community and pursue ongoing learning opportunities.

CHAPTER ELEVEN

UPCOMING DEVELOPMENTS AND TRENDS

NEW TECHNOLOGY FOR SNAIL AGRICULTURE

Modern technology in snail farming is replacing antiquated methods with more effective and fruitful ones. One of the biggest developments is automation, as automated watering and feeding systems guarantee that snails always have access to food and water. Productivity rises and labor is reduced as a result. Furthermore, climate control technologies aid in maintaining the correct humidity and temperature in snail cages, which promotes growth and lowers mortality rates.

Snail farming also heavily relies on biotechnology. Utilizing genetic research and selective breeding methods, new snail breeds with increased growth rates, disease resistance, and superior meat and slime quality are being created. Farmers may now generate more robust and profitable snail populations thanks to these developments. Furthermore, without the need for dangerous chemicals, advances in pest control technologies—like biological pest management—help shield snail farms from diseases and predators.

Farm management is being revolutionized by digital monitoring technologies and data analytics. Farmers can now track snail health, growth rates, and environmental variables in real time using sensors and software. With the help of this data-driven method, farming techniques may be precisely adjusted to maximize the health and productivity of snails. By incorporating this technology, snail farmers can achieve more efficiency, better product quality, and enhanced revenue.

ECO-FRIENDLY METHODS FOR SNAIL AGRICULTURE

For snail farming to be profitable and environmentally healthy over the long run, sustainable farming methods are crucial. Using feed that is locally obtained and organic is one essential procedure. Farmers can minimize their ecological footprint and encourage healthy nail growth by utilizing naturally occurring feed materials that are readily available in their area instead of artificial chemicals. Recycling nutrients back into the farm ecosystem, composting snail feces, and using it as a natural fertilizer for crops improve sustainability even more.

Another important component of sustainable snail farming is water conservation. Using water-saving methods, including rainwater collection and drip irrigation, can help cut down on waste and water use. Effective water management techniques preserve the ideal moisture content required for snail health while simultaneously conserving resources. Furthermore, installing water recycling technologies on the farm can save operating expenses and improve sustainability even more.

Sustainable snail farming depends on the protection of habitat and the enhancement of biodiversity. Farmers can accomplish this by utilizing polyculture methods, in which snails are raised alongside other suitable species, and by preserving the natural vegetation surrounding snail pens. This method lowers the chance of insect outbreaks, improves biodiversity, and mimics natural ecosystems.

Sustainable snail farming methods increase the farm's resilience and productivity while also helping to conserve the environment.

CONSUMER PREFERENCES AND MARKET TRENDS

Due to shifting customer preferences and growing knowledge of the health advantages of consuming snails, the market for snail products is changing. The market for premium organic snail products is expanding as customers become more aware of the foods they eat. Low in fat and high in protein, snail meat is becoming more and more well-liked as a healthful substitute for conventional meats. Furthermore, because of its restorative qualities, snail slime is becoming more and more sought after in the skincare and cosmetics sector.

Additionally, consumers are demonstrating a preference for snails raised sustainably. Labels and certifications attesting to environmentally and humanely sustainable farming methods are increasingly weighing heavily on consumer choices. Farmers can reach premium markets and command greater prices for their produce by using sustainable practices and obtaining the necessary certifications. More snail farmers are being inspired by this trend to use ethical and ecologically responsible farming practices.

Another significant trend in the market is the diversification of snail goods. Snails are being used in upscale meals, snacks, and even dietary supplements, going beyond their customary culinary applications. Businesses that raise snails are also investigating value-added goods like cosmetics and medications made from snails. Snail farmers can enhance their sources of income and fortify their enterprises by using these varied marketplaces.

RESEARCH OPPORTUNITIES AND EDUCATIONAL INITIATIVES

As the sector develops, so do educational programs and research opportunities in snail farming. Farmers can adopt best practices and increase productivity by using the knowledge and skills that training programs and workshops offer. These programs frequently address issues including disease control, sustainable farming methods, and breeding strategies. Farmers can improve their farming operations and stay up to date on the newest developments by taking part in these programs.

Universities and research centers are concentrating more and more on snail farming, investigating many facets of snail biology, diet, and farming practices. The goal of genetic and breeding studies on snails is to create better snail breeds that are resistant to disease and have faster development rates. To maximize nutrition and cut expenses, research are also being conducted on snail feed compositions.

Researcher-farmer collaboration is essential to converting scientific discoveries into useful uses on farms.

Furthermore, the provision of continuous assistance to snail farmers and the dissemination of research findings are made possible by extension services and consulting programs. These services help farmers overcome obstacles and enhance their procedures by providing them with individualized advice and troubleshooting support. Snail farmers can improve the quality of their agricultural output, expand their knowledge, and embrace innovative practices by making use of research possibilities and educational efforts.

WORLDWIDE PROSPECTS FOR SNAIL PRODUCERS

With the increasing demand for snail goods in international markets, there are more and more prospects for snail farmers worldwide. There are great prospects to export slime and snail meat to high-demand areas including Europe, Asia, and North America.

By fulfilling international quality standards and receiving the required certifications, farmers can access these markets. Farmers can establish connections with possible distributors and buyers by taking part in international trade events and exhibitions.

An additional efficient strategy for snail farmers to reach a worldwide audience is to invest in internet sales platforms. Farmers can expand their customer base and earnings potential by marketing their products outside of their local markets through e-commerce platforms and direct-to-consumer sales channels.

Establishing a robust digital footprint, comprising an intuitive website and dynamic social media accounts, can augment visibility and draw in global clientele.

Snail farmers can expand their worldwide potential by working with foreign research and development groups. These partnerships may result in information sharing, technological transfer, and financial opportunities for creative enterprises. Snail growers may remain on top of industry advances and profit from new trends by forming worldwide networks and partnerships. Businesses that engage in snail farming can greatly increase their development and profitability by seizing worldwide prospects.

www.ingramcontent.com/pod-product-compliance
Lightning Source LLC
Chambersburg PA
CBHW071836210526
45479CB00001B/159